THE POWER
OF YOUR
SUBCONSCIOUS
MIND

Also available in the Condensed Classics Library

A MESSAGE TO GARCIA

ACRES OF DIAMONDS

ALCOHOLICS ANONYMOUS

AS A MAN THINKETH

HOW TO ATTRACT GOOD LUCK

HOW TO ATTRACT MONEY

PUBLIC SPEAKING TO WIN!

SELF-RELIANCE

THE GAME OF LIFE AND HOW TO PLAY IT

THE KYBALION

THE LAW OF SUCCESS

THE MAGIC LADDER TO SUCCESS

THE MAGIC OF BELIEVING

THE MASTER KEY TO RICHES

THE MASTER MIND

THE MILLION DOLLAR SECRET HIDDEN IN YOUR MIND

THE POWER OF CONCENTRATION

THE POWER OF YOUR SUBCONSCIOUS MIND

THE SCIENCE OF BEING GREAT

THE SCIENCE OF GETTING RICH

THE SECRET DOOR TO SUCCESS

THE SECRET OF THE AGES

THINK AND GROW RICH

YOUR FAITH IS YOUR FORTUNE

THE POWER OF YOUR SUBCONSCIOUS MIND

by Joseph Murphy

The Original Classic

Abridged and Introduced
by Mitch Horowitz

THE CONDENSED CLASSICS LIBRARY™

MEDIA

Published by Gildan Media LLC
aka G&D Media.
www.GandDmedia.com

The Power of Your Subconscious Mind was originally published in 1963
G&D Media Condensed Classics edition published 2018
Abridgement and Introduction copyright © 2015 by Mitch Horowitz

FIRST EDITION: 2018

Cover design by David Rheinhardt of Pyrographx

Interior design by Meghan Day Healey of Story Horse, LLC.

ISBN: 978-1-7225-0041-2

CONTENTS

INTRODUCTION
The Power of Thought......................................9

CHAPTER ONE
The Treasure House Within You...............13

CHAPTER TWO
How Your Mind Works 15

CHAPTER THREE
**The Miracle-Working Power
of Your Subconscious Mind** 17

CHAPTER FOUR
Prayer and Your Subconscious Mind........19

CHAPTER FIVE
How to Get the Results You Want...........23

CHAPTER SIX

**How to Use Your
Subconscious Mind for Wealth** 25

CHAPTER SEVEN

**Your Subconscious Mind
as a Partner in Career Success** 29

CHAPTER EIGHT

**The Inventiveness of
Your Subconscious Mind** 31

CHAPTER NINE

**Your Subconscious Mind
and Marital Problems** 33

CHAPTER TEN

**Your Subconscious Mind
and Happiness** 37

CHAPTER ELEVEN

**Your Subconscious Mind
and Harmonious Relationships** 39

CHAPTER TWELVE
**How Your Subconscious Mind
Removes Mental Blocks**................................ 43

CHAPTER THIRTEEN
How to Stay Young in Spirit Forever........ 47

ABOUT THE AUTHORS 49

The Power of Thought

This may be one of the most personally important books you ever encounter. I say that not because I agree with every one of its premises or ideas. But, rather, because author and New Thought minister Joseph Murphy identifies and expands upon one immensely important and undervalued principle: *What you think dramatically affects your quality of life.*

This idea has been restated from antiquity to the present. John Milton put it this way in *Paradise Lost*: "The mind is its own place, and in it self can make a Heav'n of Hell, a Hell of Heav'n."

Murphy presents this principle as an absolute. He argues that thought governs health, finances, relationships, and all facets of life. I am personally unconvinced that *every* element of existence yields to thought alone. But within the folds of this idea—that mind is the master builder—can be found great truths. They are yours to discover, test, and benefit from. All that is required is to change how you think.

Murphy's philosophy is profoundly simple—but it is not for the weak or myopic. If you take seriously what you find in this book—and I urge you to—you will discover that redirecting your thoughts toward resiliency and constructiveness requires a lifetime of effort. But it is a task worthy of every motivated, mature person.

You will also learn that your emotions must be brought into play for any real self-change to occur. Emotion is more powerful than thought—never confuse or conflate the two. The mind says, "be satisfied with your portion"—emotion shouts, "I want more!" The mind says, "be calm"—emotion wants to run away. The mind says, "I'm happy for my neighbor"—emotion feels envy. Murphy supplies exercises to help align your emotions and thoughts in pursuit of a personal goal.

Murphy's message that *new thought means new life* has touched countless people since this book first appeared in 1963. This is not because Murphy's outlook is cloying or wishful; but because it is essentially true. We *all* feel that we should be practicing more dignified, generous, and self-respecting patterns of thought, tones of speech, and person-to-person relations. We harbor the conviction that we are *not* leading the lives we should be—that our abilities are underdeveloped, our decisions too hesitant and timorous, and our attitudes too selfish. Almost all of us sense the potential of a larger existence within us. This is a near-universal instinct.

The Power of Your Subconscious Mind is an instruction manual toward seeking that greater scale of life. Pay close attention to the book's principles, methods, and exercises. And, above all, *use them*.

It may be the most important step you ever take.

—Mitch Horowitz

CHAPTER ONE

The Treasure House
Within You

What, in your opinion, is the master secret of the ages? Atomic power? Thermonuclear energy? Interplanetary travel? No—not any of these. What, then, is the master secret? Where can one find it, and how can it be contacted and brought into action? The answer is extraordinarily simple. The secret is the marvelous, miracle-working power of your own subconscious mind.

You can bring into your life more ability, more health, more wealth, and more happiness by learning to contact and release the hidden forces of your subconscious.

As you follow the simple techniques in this book, you can gain the necessary knowledge and understanding to unlock your subconscious depths. Within them are infinite wisdom, infinite power, and infinite supply. Begin now to recognize these potentialities of your deeper mind, and they will take form in the world without.

The infinite intelligence within your subconscious can reveal to you everything you need to know at every moment, provided you are open-minded and receptive. You can receive new thoughts and ideas enabling you to bring forth new inventions, make new discoveries, or write plays and books. You can attract the ideal companion. You can acquire resources and wealth. You can move forward in abundance, security, joy, and dominion.

It is your *right* to discover this inner world of thought. Its miracle-working powers and eternal laws of life existed before you were born, before any religion or church appeared, and before the world itself came into being. It is with these thoughts that I urge you in the following chapters to lay hold of this wonderful, magical, transforming power that is your subconscious mind.

Chapter Two

How Your Mind Works

There are two levels of mind, conscious and subconscious. You think with your rational, conscious mind—and whatever you habitually think seeps down into your subconscious mind, which creates according to the nature of your thoughts.

Once the subconscious mind accepts an idea, it begins to execute it. Your subconscious does not engage in *proving* whether your thoughts are good or bad, but responds according to the *nature* of your thoughts or suggestions. If you consciously assume something is true, even though it may be false, your subconscious will accept it and proceed to bring about results that must necessarily follow.

Your conscious mind is the "watchman at the gate." Its chief function is to protect your subconscious from false impressions. You now know one of the basic laws of mind: Your subconscious is amenable to *suggestion*.

From infancy on, many of us have been given negative suggestions. Not knowing how to thwart them, we unconsciously accepted them. Here are some of the negative suggestions: "You can't." "You'll never amount to anything." "You'll fail." "You haven't got a chance." "It's no use." "It's not what you know, but who you know." "You're too old now." And so on.

If you look back, you can easily recall how parents, friends, relatives, teachers, and associates contributed to a campaign of negative suggestions. Study the things said to you, and you will discover that much of it was said to control you or instill fear in you. Check regularly on the negative suggestions that people make to you today. You do not have to be influenced by destructive suggestion.

Never say: "I can't." Overcome fear of failure by substituting the following statement: *I can do all things through the power of my subconscious mind.*

Never allow others to think for you. Choose your own thoughts, and make your own decisions. Always remember that *you have the capacity to choose.* Choose life! Choose love! Choose health! Choose happiness! Whatever your conscious mind assumes and believes, your subconscious mind accepts and brings to pass.

CHAPTER THREE

The Miracle-Working Power of Your Subconscious Mind

The power of your subconscious mind is enormous. It inspires you, guides you, and reveals to you names, facts, and scenes from the storehouse of memory.

Your subconscious mind never sleeps or rests. You can discover its miracle-working power by plainly stating to your subconscious prior to sleep that you wish to accomplish a certain thing. You will be delighted to find that forces within you will be released, leading to the desired answer or result.

William James, the father of American psychology, said that the power to move the world resides within your subconscious mind. Your subconscious is at one with infinite intelligence and boundless wisdom. It is fed by hidden springs. The law of life operates through it. Whatever you impress upon your subconscious, it will move heaven and earth to bring it to pass. You must, therefore, impress it with right ideas and constructive thoughts.

What is your idea or feeling about yourself right now? Every part of your being expresses that idea. Your body, vitality, finances, friends, and social status are a perfect reflection of the idea you have of yourself. What is impressed in your subconscious mind is expressed in all phases of your life.

Worry, anxiety, and fear can interfere with the normal rhythm of your heart, lungs, and other organs. Feed your subconscious mind with thoughts of harmony, health, and peace, and all the functions of your body will become normal again.

Feel the thrill of accomplishment, imagine the happy ending or solution to your problem, and what you imagine and feel will be accepted by your subconscious mind and brought to pass. The life principle will flow through you rhythmically and harmoniously as you consciously affirm: *I believe that the subconscious power that gave me this desire is now fulfilling it through me.*

Your subconscious mind can and will accomplish as much as you allow it to.

CHAPTER FOUR

Prayer and Your Subconscious Mind

I n building the Golden Gate Bridge, the chief engineer understood mathematical principles, stresses, and strains. Secondly, he had a picture of the ideal bridge across the bay. The third step was his application of tried and proven methods, which were implemented until the bridge took form. Likewise, there exist techniques and methods by which your prayers are actualized.

Prayer is the formulation of an idea concerning something you wish to accomplish. Your desire *is* your prayer. It comes out of your deepest needs and it reveals what you want in life. *Blessed are they that hunger and thirst after righteousness: for they shall be filled.* That is really prayer: life's hunger and thirst for peace, harmony, health, joy, and other blessings.

We will now explore the "passing over" technique for impregnating the subconscious mind with your desire. This involves inducing the subconscious to *take over* your prayer request as handed it by the conscious mind. This *passing over* is best accomplished in a reverie-like state. Know that within your deeper mind exist infinite intelligence and infinite power. Just calmly think over what you want; and see it coming into fuller fruition from this moment forward.

Your prayer—*your mental act*—must be accepted as an image in your mind before the power of your subconscious will play upon it and make it operative. You must reach a point of *acceptance* in your mind, an unqualified and undisputed state of agreement.

This contemplation should be accompanied by a feeling of joy and restfulness in foreseeing the accomplishment of your desire. The basis for the art and science of true prayer is your knowledge and complete confidence that the movement of your conscious mind will gain a definite response from your subconscious mind.

The easiest and most obvious way to formulate an idea is to visualize it, to see it in your mind's eye as vividly as if it were alive. You can see with the naked eye only what already exists in the external world; in a similar way, that which you can visualize in your mind's eye *already exists* in the infinite realms of thought. Any picture that you have in your mind is *the substance of things hoped for and the evidence of things not seen*. What you form in your imagination is as real as any part of your body.

Your ideas and thoughts are *real*—and will one day appear in the objective world if you remain faithful to your mental image.

CHAPTER FIVE

How to Get the Results You Want

The principle reasons for failure when trying to tap your subconscious are: 1) lack of confidence, and 2) too much effort.

Many people block answers to their prayers by failing to fully comprehend the nature of their subconscious. When you know how your mind functions, you gain a measure of *confidence*. You must remember that whenever your subconscious accepts an idea, it immediately begins to execute it. It uses all its mighty resources to that end, and mobilizes all the mental and spiritual faculties of your deeper mind. This law is true for good ideas or bad. Consequently, if you use it negatively, it brings trouble, failure, and confusion. When you use it constructively, it brings guidance, freedom, and peace.

The right answer is inevitable when your thoughts are constructive and loving. The only thing you have to do to overcome failure is to get your subconscious to accept your idea or request by *feeling its reality now*, and the law of your mind will do the rest. Turn over the request with faith and confidence, and your subconscious will take over and see it through.

You will always fail to get results by trying to use *mental coercion*—your subconscious does not respond to coercion; it responds to your faith or conscious-mind acceptance. Relaxation is the key. *Easy does it*. Do not be concerned with details and means, but rest in the assured end.

Feeling is the touchstone of all subconscious demonstration. Your new idea must be *felt subjectively*, not in the future but in a finished state, as coming about now. Get the *feel* of the happy solution to your problem. Remember how you felt in the past when you solved a major problem or recovered from a serious illness. Live in this feeling, and your subconscious depths will bring it to pass.

CHAPTER SIX

How to Use Your Subconscious Mind for Wealth

Wealth is a subconscious conviction on the part of the individual. You will not become a millionaire by saying, "I am a millionaire, I am a millionaire." Rather, you will *grow into a wealth consciousness* by building into your mentality the idea of wealth and abundance.

Perhaps you are saying to yourself now, "I need wealth and success." Follow these steps: Repeat for about five minutes to yourself three or four times a day, "Wealth—Success." These words have tremendous power. They represent the inner power of the subconscious. Anchor your mind on this substantial power within you; then corresponding conditions and circumstances will be manifested in your life.

Again, you are not merely saying, "I am wealthy." You are dwelling on real powers within you. There is no conflict in the mind when you say, "Wealth." Furthermore, the *feeling* of wealth will well up within you as you dwell on the idea of wealth.

I have talked to many people during the past thirty-five years whose usual complaint is: "I have said for weeks and months, 'I am wealthy, I am prosperous,' and nothing has happened." I discovered that when they said, "I am prosperous, I am wealthy," they felt within that they were lying to themselves. One man told me, "I have affirmed that I am prosperous until I am tired. Things are now worse. I knew when I made that statement that it was obviously not true." His statements were rejected by the conscious mind, and the very opposite of what he outwardly affirmed was made manifest.

Your affirmation succeeds best when it is specific and when it does not produce a mental conflict or argument; hence, the statements made by this man made matters worse because they suggested his lack. Your subconscious mind accepts what you really feel to be true, not just idle words or statements.

Here is the ideal way to overcome this conflict. Make this statement frequently, particularly prior to sleep: *By day and by night I am being prospered in all of my interests.* This affirmation will not arouse any argument because it does not contradict your subconscious mind's impression of financial lack.

Many people tell themselves, "I deserve a higher salary." I believe that most people are, in fact, underpaid. One reason why many people do not have more money is that they are silently or openly condemning it. They call money "filthy lucre" or say "love of money is the root of all evil." Another reason they do not prosper is that they have a sneaky subconscious feeling that there is some virtue in poverty. This subconscious pattern may be due to early childhood training, superstition, or a mistaken interpretation of Scripture

Cleanse your mind of all conflicting beliefs about money. Do not regard money as evil or filthy. If you do, you cause it to take wings and fly away from you. You lose what you condemn.

At the same time, do not make a god of money. It is only a symbol. Remember that the real riches are in your mind. You are here to lead a balanced life—and that includes acquiring all the money you need.

There is one emotion that causes lack of wealth in the lives of many. Most people learn this the hard way. It is envy. To entertain envious thoughts is devastating; it places you in a negative position in which wealth flows *from* you rather than *to* you. If you are ever annoyed or irritated by the prosperity of another, claim immediately that you truly wish him greater wealth in every possible way. This will neutralize your negative thoughts, and cause an ever-greater measure of wealth to flow to you.

CHAPTER SEVEN

Your Subconscious Mind as a Partner in Career Success

L et us discuss three steps to success. The first step is to discover the thing you love to do, and then do it. Success is in loving your work.

Some may say, "How can I put the first step into operation? I do not know what I should do." In such a case, pray for guidance as follows: *The infinite intelligence of my subconscious mind reveals to me my true place in life*. Repeat this prayer quietly, positively, and lovingly to your deeper mind. As you persist with faith and confidence, the answer will come to you as a feeling, a hunch, or a tendency in a certain direction. It will come to you clearly and in peace, as an inner awareness.

The second step to success is to specialize in some particular branch of work, and to know more about it than anyone else. For example, if a young man chooses chemistry as his profession, he should concentrate on one of the many branches in that field. He should give all of his time and attention to his chosen specialty. He should become sufficiently enthusiastic to know all there is about it; if possible, he should know more than anyone else.

The third step is the most important. You must be certain that the thing you want to do does not build your success only. *Your desire must not be selfish; it must benefit humanity.* The path of a complete circuit must be formed. In other words, your idea must go forth with the purpose of blessing or serving the world. It will then come back to you pressed down, shaken together, and running over. If it is to benefit you alone, the circle or circuit is not formed.

A successful person loves his work and expresses himself fully. True success is contingent upon a higher ideal than mere accumulation of riches. The person of success is one who possesses great psychological and spiritual understanding, and whose work benefits others.

CHAPTER EIGHT

The Inventiveness of Your Subconscious Mind

Nikola Tesla was a brilliant electrical scientist who brought forth amazing inventions in the late-nineteenth and early twentieth centuries. When an idea for a new invention entered Tesla's mind, he would build it up in his imagination, knowing that his subconscious would construct and reveal to his conscious mind all the parts needed for its manufacture. Through quietly contemplating every possible improvement, he spent no time in correcting defects, and was able to give technicians perfect plans for the product.

"Invariably," he said, "my device works as I imagined it should. In twenty years there has not been a single exception."

When you have what you term "a difficult decision" to make, or when you fail to see the solution to a problem, begin at once to think constructively about it. If you are fearful and worried, you are not really thinking. True thinking is free from fear.

Here is a simple technique to receive inner guidance on any subject: Quiet the mind and still the body. Go to a quiet place where you won't be disturbed—preferably lying on a bed, sofa, or in a recliner. Mobilize your attention; focus your thoughts on the solution to the problem. Try to solve it with your conscious mind. Think how happy you would be with the perfect solution. Sense the feeling you would have if the right answer were yours now. Let your mind play with this mood in a relaxed way; then drop off to sleep. When you awaken, and do not have the answer, get busy about something else. When you are preoccupied with something else, the answer will probably come into your mind like toast pops from out of a toaster.

The secret of guidance or right action is to mentally devote yourself to the right answer, until you find its response in you. The response is a feeling, an inner awareness, and an overpowering hunch whereby *you know that you know*. In such cases, you have used the infinite power of your subconscious to the point where *it begins to use you*. You cannot fail or make a false step while operating under the subconscious wisdom within you.

CHAPTER NINE

Your Subconscious Mind and Marital Problems

Recently a young couple, married for only a few months, was seeking a divorce. I discovered that the young man had a constant fear that his wife would leave him. He expected rejection, and he believed that she would be unfaithful. These thoughts haunted him and became an obsession. His mental attitude was one of separation and suspicion. His own feeling of loss and separation operated through the relationship. This brought about a condition in accordance with the mental pattern behind it.

His wife left home and asked for a divorce, which is what he feared and believed would happen.

Divorce occurs first in the mind; the legal proceedings follow. These two young people were full of resentment, fear, suspicion, and anger. These attitudes weaken and debilitate the whole being. The couple began to realize what they had been doing with their minds. These two people returned together at my suggestion and experimented with *prayer therapy*, a method we will learn.

Each one practiced radiating to the other love, peace, harmony, health, and good will. They alternated in reading the Psalms every night. Their marriage began growing more beautiful every day.

Now, divorce is an individual problem. It cannot be generalized. In some cases, no marriage should have occurred to begin with. In other cases, divorce is not the solution. Divorce may be right for one person and wrong for another. A divorced woman may be far more sincere and noble than many of her married sisters, who are perhaps living a lie.

For couples that wish to *stay together* the solution is to *pray together*. Here is a three-step program in prayer therapy.

FIRST

Never carry over from one day to another accumulated irritations arising from little disappointments. Forgive each other for any sharpness before you retire at night. The moment you awaken, claim infinite intelligence is guiding you in all ways. Send out thoughts of peace, harmony, and love to your partner, to all family members, and to the entire world.

SECOND

Say grace at breakfast. Give thanks for the wonderful food, for your abundance, and for all your blessings. Make sure that no problems, worries, or arguments enter into the table conversation; the same applies at dinnertime. Say to your partner, "I appreciate all you are doing, and I radiate love and good will to you all day long."

THIRD

Spouses should alternate in praying each night. Do not take your marriage partner for granted. Show your appreciation and love. Think appreciation and good will, rather than condemnation, criticism, and nagging. Before going to sleep read the 23rd, 27th, and 91st Psalms; the 11th chapter of Hebrews; the 13th chapter of I Corinthians; and other great texts of the Bible.

As you practice these steps, your marriage will grow more blessed through the years.

CHAPTER TEN

Your Subconscious Mind and Happiness

There is a phrase in the Bible: *Choose ye this day whom ye will serve.*

You have the freedom to *choose happiness.* This may seem extraordinarily simple—and it is. Perhaps this is why so many people stumble over the way to happiness; they do not see the simplicity of the key to happiness. The great things of life are simple, dynamic, and creative.

St. Paul reveals how you can think your way into a life of dynamic power and happiness in these words: *Finally, brethren, whatsoever things are true, whatsoever things are honest, whatsoever things are just, whatsoever things are pure, whatsoever things are lovely, whatsoever things are of good report; if there be any virtue, and if there be any praise, think on these things.* (Philippians 4:8)

There is one very important point about being happy. You must sincerely *desire* to be happy. Some people have been depressed, dejected, and unhappy for so long that when they are suddenly made happy by some joyous news they actually feel uncomfortable. They have become so accustomed to the old mental patterns that they do not feel at home being happy. They long for the familiar depressed state.

Begin now to choose happiness. Here is how: When you open your eyes in the morning, say to yourself: *Divine order takes charge of my life today and every day. All things work together for good for me today. This is a new and wonderful day for me. There will never be another day like this one. I am divinely guided all day long, and whatever I do will prosper. Divine love surrounds me, enfolds me, and enwraps me, and I go forth in peace. Whenever my attention wanders away from what is good and constructive, I will immediately bring it back to the contemplation of that which is lovely and of good report. I am a spiritual and mental magnet attracting to myself all things that bless and prosper me. I am going to be a wonderful success in all my undertakings today. I am definitely going to be happy all day long.*

Start each day in this manner; you will then be choosing happiness.

Your Subconscious Mind and Harmonious Relationships

Matthew 7:12 says, *All things whatsoever ye would that men should do unto you, do ye even so to them.*

This passage has outer and inner meanings. We are interested in its inner meaning, which is: As you would that men should *think* about you, think about them. As you would that men should *feel* about you, feel about them. As you would want men to *act* toward you, act toward them.

For example, you may be polite and courteous to someone in your office, but inside you are critical and resentful. Such negative thoughts are highly destructive to you. You are actually taking mental poisons, which rob you of enthusiasm, strength, guidance, and good will. These negative thoughts and emotions sink into your subconscious, and cause you all kinds of difficulties and maladies.

Matthew 7:1-2 says, *Judge not, that ye not be judged. For with what judgment ye judge, ye shall be judged; and with what measure ye shall mete, it shall be measured to you again.*

The study and application of these verses, and their inner truth, provides the key to harmonious relations. To judge is to think, to reach a mental verdict or conclusion in your mind. Your thoughts are creative, therefore, you actually create in your own experience what you think and feel about another person. It is also true that the suggestion you give to another, you give to yourself.

Now, there *are* difficult people in the world who are twisted and distorted mentally. They are malconditioned. Many are mental delinquents, argumentative, uncooperative, cantankerous, and cynical. They are sick psychologically. Many people have deformed and distorted minds, probably warped during childhood. Many have congenital deformities. You would not condemn a person who had tuberculosis, nor should you condemn someone who is mentally ill. You should have compassion and understanding. *To understand all is to forgive all.*

At the same time, do not permit people to take advantage of you and gain their point by temper tantrums, crying jags, or so-called heart attacks. These people are dictators who try to enslave you and make you do their bidding. Be firm but kind, and refuse to yield. *Appeasement never wins.* You are here to fulfill your ideal and to remain true to the eternal verities and spiritual values of life.

Give no one the power to deflect you from your goal, your aim in life, which is to express your hidden talents to the world, to serve humanity, and to reveal more and more of God's wisdom, truth, and beauty. Know definitely that whatever contributes to your peace, happiness, and fulfillment must, of necessity, bless all who walk the earth. The harmony of the part is the harmony of the whole, for the whole is in the part, and the part in the whole.

CHAPTER TWELVE

How Your Subconscious Mind Removes Mental Blocks

A young man asked Socrates how he could get wisdom. Socrates replied, "Come with me." He took the lad to a river, pushed the boy's head under the water, held it there until the boy was gasping for air, then relaxed and released his head. When the boy regained his composure, the teacher asked, "What did you desire most when you were under water?"

"I wanted air," said the boy.

Socrates told him, "When you want wisdom as much as you wanted air, you will receive it."

Likewise, when you possess an intense desire to overcome any block or addiction, and you reach a clear-cut decision that there is a way out, and that is the course you wish to follow, then victory and triumph are assured.

If you are an alcoholic or drug addict, begin by admitting it. Do not dodge the issue. Many people remain alcoholics because they refuse to admit it. If you have a burning desire to free yourself from any destructive habit, you are fifty-one percent healed. When you have a greater desire to give up a habit than to continue it, you will gain complete freedom.

Whatever thought you anchor the mind upon, the mind magnifies. If you engage the mind on the concept of freedom from habit and peace of mind, you generate feelings that gradually emotionalize the concept of freedom and peace. Whatever idea you emotionalize is accepted by your subconscious and brought to pass.

Use these steps to help cope with addiction:

FIRST
Get still; quiet the wheels of the mind. Enter into a sleepy, drowsy state. In this relaxed, peaceful, receptive state you are preparing for the second step.

SECOND
Take a brief phrase, which can readily be graven on the memory, and repeat it over and over as a lullaby. Use the phrase: *Sobriety and peace of mind are mine now, and I give thanks.* To prevent the mind from wandering, repeat the phrase aloud or sketch its pronunciation with

your lips and tongue as you say it mentally. This helps its entry into your subconscious. Do this for five minutes or more. You will find a deep emotional response.

THIRD

Just before going to sleep, imagine a friend or loved one in front of you. Your eyes closed, you are relaxed and at peace. The loved one or friend is subjectively present, and is saying to you, "Congratulations!" You see the smile; you hear the voice. You mentally touch the hand; it is all vivid and real. The word "congratulations" implies *complete freedom*. Hear it over and over until you get the subconscious reaction that satisfies.

CHAPTER THIRTEEN

How to Stay Young in Spirit Forever

Your subconscious never grows old. It is part of the universal mind of God, which was never born and will never die.

Patience, kindness, veracity, humility, good will, harmony, and brotherly love are eternal attributes, which never age. If you continue to generate these qualities, you will remain young in spirit.

During my many years of public life, I have studied the careers of famous people who have continued their productivity well beyond the normal span of life. Some achieved their greatness in old age. I have also met and known countless individuals of no prominence who, in their lesser sphere, belong to those hardy mortals who have proven that old age of itself does not destroy the creative powers of the mind and body.

My father learned French at sixty-five, and became an authority on it at seventy. He made a study of Gaelic when he was over sixty, and became a well-regarded teacher of the subject. He assisted my sister in a school of higher learning and continued to do so until he passed away at ninety-nine. His mind was as clear at ninety-nine as it was at twenty. Moreover, his handwriting and reasoning powers improved with age.

A Hollywood screenwriter told me that he had to write scripts that would cater to the twelve-year-old mind. This is a tragic state of affairs if the great masses of people are expected to be emotionally and spiritually mature. It means the emphasis is placed on youth in spite of how youth stands for inexperience, lack of discernment, and hasty judgment.

Old age really means the contemplation of the truths of God from the highest standpoint. Realize that you are on an endless journey, a series of important steps in the ceaseless, tireless, endless ocean of life. Then, with the Psalmist, you will say, *They shall still bring forth fruit in old age; they shall be fat and flourishing.* (Psalm 92:14)

You are a child of Infinite Life, which knows no end, a child of Eternity.

Joseph Murphy was born in 1898 on the southern coast of Ireland. Raised in a devout Catholic family, Murphy had planned on joining the priesthood. As young man he instead relocated to America to make his career as a chemist and druggist. After running a pharmacy counter at New York's Algonquin Hotel, Murphy began studying mystical and metaphysical ideas. In the 1940s he became a popular New Thought minister and writer. Murphy wrote prolifically on the autosuggestive and mystical faculties of the human mind. He became widely known for his metaphysical classic, *The Power of Your Subconscious Mind*, which has sold millions of copies since it first appeared in 1963. Considered one of the pioneering voices of New Thought and affirmative-thinking philosophy, Murphy died in Laguna Hills, California, in 1981.

Mitch Horowitz, who abridged and introduced this volume, is the PEN Award-winning author of books including *Occult America* and *The Miracle Club: How Thoughts Become Reality*. *The Washington Post* says

Mitch "treats esoteric ideas and movements with an even-handed intellectual studiousness that is too often lost in today's raised-voice discussions." Follow him @MitchHorowitz.

Printed in the USA
CPSIA information can be obtained
at www.ICGtesting.com
JSHW012046140824
68134JS00034B/3295

9 781722 500412